MW01131623

WRITERS REPUBLIC

JESUS LOVES You So Much

Coloring Book

Story by: Toni McNeil

WRITERS REPUBLIC L.L.C.
515 Summit Ave. Unit R1
Union City, NJ 07087, USA

Website: *www.writersrepublic.com*
Hotline: *1-877-656-6838*
Email: *info@writersrepublic.com*

Ordering Information:
Quantity sales. Special discounts are available on quantity purchases by corporations, associations, and others. For details, contact the publisher at the address above.

Library of Congress Control Number:	2020951960	
ISBN-13:	978-1-63728-041-6	[Paperback Edition]
	978-1-63728-042-3	[Digital Edition]

Rev. date: 12/11/2020

To my heavenly Father for always exceeding my expectations and pushing me beyond my abilities. All the glory belongs to him.

To my husband Patrick Mcneil for always believing in me and pushing me to follow my dreams no matter how big they seem. Thanks for your unconditional love and support. I could not have done any of this without you. I love you!

To my children Patrick, Patrick Jr., and Patrecia . Thanks for your encouragement and support. I love you all.

To my siblings Viquita, Emjay, Daniel, and Donald. Thanks for all your encouragement and support. I love you all. To my spiritual mother Minister Debby Osei that spoke a prophetic word over me on 4/18/20 that I would begin writing a series of children's books. Thanks for praying, believing and standing with me through it all. You are the real deal and I love you.

To all my friends that encouraged me and cheered me on: Jaleesa Dunn, Henrietta Koon, Kaneta Alexander, Marla Garrett, Lakeva Williams, Carla Willis ,Tonja Carter, Stacy Mack, Andre Sheppard and Shanda Davis. I love you all and thanks for everything.

2

Jesus loves you so much that he sent his only son to die on the cross for you.

John 3:16

Jesus loves you so much that he sends his angels to protect you.

Psalm 91:11

Jesus loves you so much that he already has a plan for your life.

Jeremiah 29:11

Jesus loves you so much that he heals you when you are sick.

Psalm 103:3

Jesus loves you so much that he knows how many hairs are on your head.

Luke 12:7

Jesus loves you so much that he will never leave you.

Deuteronomy 31:8

Jesus Loves you
so much that he
forgives you.

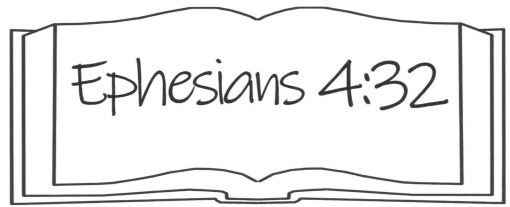

Ephesians 4:32

Jesus loves you so much that he hears and answers your prayers.

Jeremiah 29:12

Jesus loves you so much because you were created just like him.

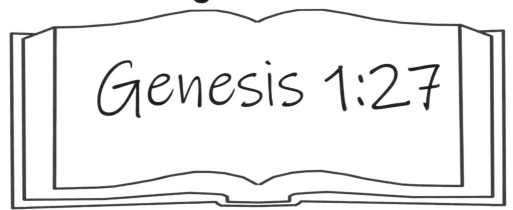

Genesis 1:27

You have a special place in God's heart

Jeremiah 1:5

Scripture reference

Easy-to-Read Version

Page 3: John 3:16 Yes, God loved the world so much that he gave his only son, so that everyone who believes in him would not be lost but have eternal life.

Page 5: Psalm 91:11 He will command his angels to protect you wherever you go.

Page 7: Jeremiah 29:11 I say this because I know the plans that I have for you. "This message is from the Lord. "I have good plans for you. I don't plan to hurt you. I plan to give you hope and a good future.

Page 9: Psalms 103:3 He forgives all our sins and heals all our sicknesses.

Page 11: Luke 12:7 Yes, God even knows how many hairs you have on your head. Don't be afraid. You are worth much more than many birds.

Page 13: Deuteronomy 31:8 The Lord will lead you. He himself is with you. He will not fail you or leave you. Don't worry. Don't be afraid.

Page 15: Ephesians 4:32 Be kind and loving to each other. Forgive each other the same as God forgave you through Christ.

Page 17: Jeremiah 29:12 Then you will call my name. You will come to me and pray to me, and I will listen to you.

Page 19 : Genesis 1:27 So God created humans in his own image. He created then to be like himself. He created them male and female.

Page 21: Jeremiah 1:5 Before I made you in your mother's wound. I knew you. Before you were born. I chose you for a special work. I chose you to be a prophet to the nations

Contact the Author

Toni McNeil

P.O. Box 55 Haslet Texas 76052

Email: Jesuslovesyouforu@gmail.com

CPSIA information can be obtained
at www.ICGtesting.com
Printed in the USA
LVHW071113070121
675635LV00002B/13